Talyllyn
Reflections

Remembering The Talyllyn Railway's 150th Anniversary Celebrations

Edited By
Ian Drummond

Holne Publishing

Contents

© Holne Publishing and Ian Drummond 2016
British Library Cataloguing in Publication Data
A record for this book is available from the British Library
ISBN 978-0-9956387-0-9
Published by: Holne Publishing, PO Box 343, LEEDS, LS19 9FW
Typesetting by: Holne Publishing Services, PO Box 343, LEEDS, LS19 9FW
Printed by: Charlesworth Press, Flanshaw Way, Flanshaw Lane, Wakefield, WF2 9LP

Holne Publishing
PO Box 343
LEEDS
LS19 9FW
enquiries@holnepublishing.co.uk
www.holnepublishing.co.uk

Cover Photos:

Front

Top: Locomotives No. 1 *Talyllyn* and No.2 *Dolgoch* at Dolgoch station with the 'The Sesquicentenarian' on Friday 3 July 2015. While the fireman waters *Talyllyn* the driver, Andrew Young, can be seen chatting with special guests Timothy West and Prunella Scales, who would assist in the burying of a time capsule at Abergynolwyn station later in the day.   (Photo: Darren Turner)

Bottom: A unique line up of locomotives at Tywyn Wharf station on Saturday 4 July during 'The 150th Party' gala. Left to right are *Russell* from the Welsh Highland Heritage Railway, which had been stored at Tywyn Wharf station between 1955 and 1965 before restoration to running order, the Ffestiniog Railway's *Prince* the oldest working narrow gauge locomotive in the world built in 1863, then *Talyllyn* built in 1864 and *Dolgoch* built in 1866.   (Photo: David J. Mitchell)

Back Page: Another unique line up of locomotives on Saturday 2 July 2016 as part of 'The Grand Finale' gala with all five of the surviving UK-based locomotives built by Fletcher, Jennings and Co. at Lowca works near Whitehaven. Left to right are *Townsend Hook* built in 1880 and now based at the Amberley Museum and Heritage Centre having been cosmetically restored. Then standard gauge locomotive *Captain Baxter* from the Bluebell Railway which was in steam on a specially laid section of track. Then the Talyllyn Railway's *Dolgoch* next to which is *William Finlay*, the twin of *Townsend Hook* also cosmetically restored having been acquired by the Narrow Gauge Railway Museum Trust at Tywyn and finally the Talyllyn Railway's No.1 *Talyllyn*.
          (Photo: Darren Turner)

Introduction

This book is a celebration of the events held to commemorate the 150th Anniversary of the Talyllyn Railway (TR), the World's First Preserved Railway, between 2014 and 2016. Some were spectacular galas, others were much smaller scale, but they all contributed to a memorable two years in the life of the railway.

Inevitably putting on such a series of events meant a lot of hard work on the part of many people. Therefore this volume is dedicated to all those who helped in whatever way to making them a success. Of course we also need to remember those early pioneers of the Talyllyn Railway Preservation Society (TRPS) Tom Rolt, Bill Trinder, Pat Whitehouse and many, many others without whom this railway would not be here today.

The early history of the Talyllyn Railway is somewhat complicated. Construction of the line began in April 1864 as a tramroad to transport slate from the Bryneglwys quarry to Tywyn. Here it was transshipped to the standard gauge Coast line for transport to its final destination, which could be on the other side of the world.

It was designed for steam power from the outset, the first railway of so narrow a gauge to be so. The first steam locomotive was completed at the Lowca Works of Fletcher, Jennings and Co. in September 1864, but It did not arrive on the railway until April 1865, when construction was virtually complete.

Above: The special Talyllyn 150 logo designed by Lel Johnson which proved to be a real hit with members and public alike.

Slate traffic commenced shortly afterwards, but an Act authorising the introduction of passenger trains did not receive its Royal Assent until 5 July 1865. Even then advertised passenger trains did not start to run until December 1866, which was despite the railway's first passenger carriage arriving in January 1866. This followed the delivery of a second locomotive in September 1866, and a second carriage probably in early December the same year.

Therefore, with such a myriad of potential dates to celebrate, it was decided that for the 150th Anniversary of the railway that rather than have just one celebration, a series of events would be held to mark some of the key dates in the railway's history, including its preservation in 1951. This would include five gala weekends in 2015, with another two subsequently being held in 2016.

These events would break new ground for the railway with never before seen sights in the railway's history. They also provided a walk through the railway's 150 year history, with events from its past brought to life in the present. However, they were also designed to be fun and to bring a smile to the faces of all those involved.

Many of the events generated major attention in the railway world demonstrating that the Talyllyn was far from resting on its laurels and indeed was ready for another 150 years of service.

The photographs reproduced here record these series of events and serve to provide a reminder of them. Inevitably, however, some aspects of the events will have been omitted due to pressures on space, but we have tried to cover as much ground as possible with the photographs available.

I am grateful to all those photographers who have contributed to this album and also to my wife Di, as well as Lawrie Bowles, Alan Doe and Andrew Young, for their help with proof reading. It is my hope that this book will be counted as a worthy souvenir of these past two years.

Ian Drummond
September 2016

Talyllyn's 150th Anniversary

The first event in the Talyllyn 150 celebrations was to mark the 150th Anniversary of locomotive No.1 *Talyllyn* on 24 September 2014. However, on 6 April 2014 the locomotive suffered a mechanical failure in service which resulted in major damage to the right hand side motion. This led to the decision to send the locomotive to the Ffestiniog Railway's Boston Lodge works at Porthmadog on 22 April 2014.

Talyllyn was transferred to Porthmadog by road. Here it was loaded onto a wagon on the Welsh Highland Railway, the difference in track gauges between the Talyllyn's 2 ft 3 in and the Ffestiniog's 1 ft 11 ½ in meaning that the locomotive could not directly run on the Ffestiniog's rails. The wagon and loco were then brought down to Porthmadog station and across the the famous Cob to Boston Lodge works.

Top Left: Repairs were completed for the locomotive to return to Tywyn on 19 August 2014 when the procedure was reversed. No.1 can be seen being propelled across Britannia bridge at Porthmadog on its return journey.

(Photo: Barbara Fuller)

Left: It was then brought back to Tywyn Wharf and unloaded in time for its 150th anniversary. (Photo: Chris Price)

Above: Locomotive No.1 *Talyllyn* breaks a banner at Tywyn Wharf on 24 September 2014 to mark its own 150th anniversary and the start of the Talyllyn Railway's 150th Anniversary celebrations. The day also saw the launch of a book by Martin Fuller, seen here driving the locomotive, tracing the pre-preservation history of the Talyllyn's locomotives. Holding the barrier are (left to right): Chris Price, then General Manager of the Railway; Jane Garvey chairman of the TRPS and David Mitchell in-coming President of the Society. (Photo: Barbara Fuller)

Above: On 28 September 2014 *Talyllyn and Dolgoch* were seen together re-enacting the events of the celebrations held a few days earlier for the benefit of members of the TRPS, as part of the Society's AGM weekend. Here they are in charge of a special mixed train at Brynglas. (Photo: Ian Drummond)

Above: At the end of November 2014 No.1 *Talyllyn* went to the Warley Model Railway Exhibition at the National Exhibition Centre in Birmingham along with original brake van No.5 to publicise the Talyllyn 150 events. Few knew it at the time but this would be the last time it would be seen in the black livery, for it and No.2 *Dolgoch* were about to undergo a remarkable transformation. (Photo: Ian Drummond)

The Surprise

Martin Fuller's research had revealed the intriguing possibility that the original livery applied to *Talyllyn* and *Dolgoch* might not have been green as long thought, but could have been Indian Red as applied to other Fletcher Jennings locomotives, and which was produced from local minerals in the Whitehaven area. It was felt that both Nos. 1 and 2 should be repainted for the 150th celebrations and so it was decided to repaint them in Indian Red liveries with lining as close as possible to the original Fletcher Jennings products. The repainting was carried out by Heritage Painting in top secrecy in December 2014 and the results revealed to the world on Christmas Day. The photos caused a sensation and truly made the point that the Talyllyn 150 celebrations were going to be something special.

Above: *Talyllyn* and *Dolgoch* in their new liveries at Tywyn Pendre in December 2014.   (Photo: Darren Turner)

Above: Both locos again at Tywyn Pendre showing the magnificent lining on No.1 *Talyllyn*.   (Photo: Barbara Fuller)

Right: In mid-March 2015 a series of photo charters were run featuring *Talyllyn* in its new livery. Here it is seen on Brynglas bank with a short mixed train just as it might have been in the early years of the railway.

(Photo: Gareth Jones)

Below: Again on Brynglas bank, but this time *Talyllyn* is in charge of the full vintage set at twilight, with a beautiful lighting effect.   (Photo: Gareth Jones)

Right: Another event which became part of the 150th celebrations was the placing of a plaque on the site of Bill Trinder's radio shop in the High Street, Banbury. This was the place where Bill Trinder and Tom Rolt first started discussing the Talyllyn Railway, which eventually led to the founding of the World's First Railway Preservation Society in October 1950. Bill Trinder's daughter, Cynthia Turner, reads the plaque she had just unveiled on 28 March 2015. Much of the work for the installation of the plaque was done by the Banbury Civic Society.   (Photo: Ian Drummond)

The Quarryman Experience Gala
2 - 4 May 2015

Left: The first gala was 'The Quarryman Experience' held over the May Day Bank Holiday weekend in 2015. Unfortunately on the Friday night just before the gala began one of the worst storms of the year blew in and wreaked havoc. A marquee that had been erected in Dolgoch woods to serve cream teas disappeared into the trees, and the children's games, which had been scheduled to take place there, had to be cancelled.

In spite of this an intrepid group of photographers set out from Tywyn Wharf at just before 7 am on a special train behind No.1 *Talyllyn* driven by Martin Fuller. The Talyllyn 150 galas were under way.(Photo: Ian Drummond)

Above: The focus of 'The Quarryman Experience' was the early years of the railway when it was built by the Aberdovey Slate Company under the chairmanship of Thomas McConnel. Later William McConnel bought the Bryneglwys quarry and the railway, and the family continued to own both until 1911. To celebrate this on Saturday 1 May 2016 the 'McConnel Special' was run. This was also the first public appearance of No. 1 *Talyllyn* and No.2 *Dolgoch* double-heading a train since their re-paint. The train is seen departing Dolgoch in what were atrocious conditions.

(Photo: Barbara Fuller)

Above: How many heritage railways would be able to reproduce a photograph over one hundred years old with the original locomotive and rolling stock featuring the son of the original photographer? The gathering of the McConnel family was in part also to mark the launch of a book about those who worked on the Talyllyn Railway before preservation by Sara Eade. During their trip on the railway there was an attempt at a reproduction of a well-known photograph of the McConnel family taken in the late 19th century at the then limit of locomotive working, now Nant Gwernol station (below).

The original photograph was taken by William Houldsworth McConnel, whose son, Roger, stands third from the left in the group

beside the locomotive at Nant Gwernol station in the photo above. The picture does not show the intensity of the rain at this point, but a suitable reproduction of the photograph was obtained.

In the 1890s photo the locomotive driver was Bob Thomas, seen to the left of the loco. In 2015 David Jones, standing to the left of *Talyllyn*, whose family associations with the railway go back to nearly the date of the original photograph, was fulfilling the role.

(Top Photo: Ian Drummond
Bottom Photo: TR Collection)

Left: Spurred on by the reproduction of the McConnel photograph some of our volunteers were inspired to recreate some other photographs from the past. Here left to right Andrew Vick, Andrew Young and John Burton recreate a photograph (below) of No.2 Dolgoch c.1916 with, again left to right, Driver Dick Price, Loco Fitter Hugh Griffiths and Guard Jacob Rowlands.
(Photo Left: Andrew Young, Below TR collection)

Left: Another 'Edwardian' photograph this time at Tywyn Wharf with locomotives Nos.1 and 2 with left to right Ellis Jacklin, Andrew Vick and Andrew Young. (Photo: Darren Turner)

Left: Others entered into the spirit of the weekend by appearing in Victorian costume as seen here at Tywyn Wharf.
(Photo: Darren Turner)

Right: In the early days of the preserved railway there were many photos of a lady, Hanna Evans, in Welsh costume with the train at Abergynolwyn. Here her granddaughter Jennie, now a member of the railway's staff, poses next to No.4 *Edward Thomas* with the Corris mixed train at Dolgoch station. Here she had been attempting to sell cream teas, but the inclement weather meant there were few takers. Keith Hayes, the guard, is behind her.
(Photo: Darren Turner)

Below: Among the other activities on show was a display of slate splitting by Paul Perryman at Tywyn Wharf.
(Photo: Darren Turner)

Above: Another pair of 'Victorians' sample first class travel Victorian style in one of our ex-Glyn Valley Tramway carriages.
(Photo: Andrew Young)

Left: In spite of the rain there were still some excellent photo opportunities such as this one in Wharf cutting of No.2 *Dolgoch* with a slate train passing a superb display of bluebells, a feature of the line at that time of year.   (Photo: Andrew Young)

Below: Later the same train is seen at Tŷ Dŵr on the former mineral extension between Abergynolwyn and Nant Gwernol. (Photo: Barbara Fuller)

Left: Another re-creation was 'The Quarryman'. This was a named train that ran every day in the running season in the 1990s and early 2000s. It is seen here approaching Abergynolwyn with No.1 *Talyllyn* in charge. Jack Evans is the fireman.
(Photo: Barbara Fuller)

Right: Of course much of the limelight during the gala was on engines Nos. 1 and 2, but our other locomotives were not forgotten. Here No.6 *Douglas* is seen just outside Abergynolwyn station with one of the regular service trains that ran on Saturday 2 May 2015. Bill Tyndall watches from the cab.
(Photo: Andrew Young)

Left: No.4 *Edward Thomas* is seen early on Monday 4 May with a photographic special consisting of a Corris mixed train. By now the weather was improving, although typically many visitors had given up and gone home. However, some still enjoyed the Bank Holiday Monday weather along with a mini-music festival that was held on Abergynolwyn station during the day. Bill Tyndall is at the regulator and Ruth Goode can be seen through the guards van window.
(Photo: David J. Mitchell)

Right: All too soon it was time for the final departure of the gala as No. 4 *Edward Thomas* and No.7 *Tom Rolt* headed out with the 3.45 pm departure from Tywyn Wharf on Monday 4 May 2015. (Photo: Ian Drummond)

The 150th Party
3 - 5 July 2015

Left and Below: 'The 150th Party' gala broke new ground for the Talyllyn Railway. For the first time we had visiting narrow gauge locomotives in steam at Tywyn Wharf with a different gauge from our own. This was made possible by the laying of two special 2 ft gauge tracks. The preparations were made by a hard working team in the week leading up to the event, so that everything was ready for our guests.

(Photos: Diane Drummond)

Above: By Thursday 2 July 2015 everything was ready and the first of our guests had safely arrived. On the left is *Russell*, built by Hunslet for the Portmadoc, Beddgelert & South Snowdon Railway Company in 1906, which became part of the Welsh Highland Railway in 1922, and now based on the Welsh Highland Heritage Railway. Next to it is the Ffestiniog Railway's *Prince*, built in 1863 and the oldest working narrow gauge locomotive in the world. Then there is the Talyllyn Railway's No.6 *Douglas* and finally on the right No.1 *Talyllyn* which is a year younger than Prince.

(Photo: Ian Drummond)

Left: The event attracted considerable attention including a film crew from BBC *Midlands Today* who did some live broadcasts from the railway highlighting our connections to the West Midlands. Also in the photo TRPS Chairman Jane Garvey chats to one of our other special guests Timothy West.
(Photo: Diane Drummond)

Below: Timothy West then assisted TRPS President, David Mitchell in holding a banner which was broken by *Talyllyn* and *Dolgoch* at the head of 'The Sesquicentenarian' special train.
(Photo: Darren Turner)

Left: Timothy West also helped with the burying of a time capsule at Abergynolwyn station, some of the contents of which had been contributed by local school children.
(Photo: Darren Turner)

Right: The train crew (left to right: Andrew Vick, Simon Jenkins, Liz Garvey, Marc Smith and Andrew Young) pose at Tywyn Wharf with Timothy West and Prunella Scales on their return from the trip.
(Photo: Andrew Young)

Above: A dramatic view of *Russell* and *Prince* at Tywyn Wharf station.

(Photo: Darren Turner)

Above: Another historical shot with *Russell*, *Prince* and *Talyllyn* all bathing in the sunlight at Tywyn Wharf.

(Photo: Darren Turner)

Left: Up at the sheds at Pendre other preparations were also under way with *Talyllyn* being made ready under the watchful gaze of Marc Smith and Morgan Price.

(Photo: Andrew Young)

Below: On Saturday morning 4 July a special photo line up was planned with all locomotives capable of being steamed gathered at Tywyn Wharf. Here the Talyllyn Railway's then steamable fleet of No.1 *Talyllyn*, No.2 *Dolgoch*, No.4 *Edward Thomas*, No.6 *Douglas* and No.7 *Tom Rolt* are assembled at Tywyn Pendre ready for the trip to Wharf station. (Photo: Andrew Young)

Above: The arrival of the cavalcade at Wharf created the largest number of narrow gauge locomotives ever seen in steam on the Talyllyn Railway. Seven locomotives in total, when their whistles were sounded the noise was deafening! (Left to right the locomotives are: *Russell*, *Prince*, *Talyllyn*, *Dolgoch*, *Edward Thomas*, *Douglas* and *Tom Rolt*)   (Photo: Barbara Fuller)

Above: From a different angle the line up was just as interesting.   (Photo: Ian Drummond)

Left: As part of the 150th Party we also remembered more aspects of the railway's history, in particular its role as the carrier of the mails up the valley to Abergynolwyn for many years. To celebrate this we ran a 'Mail Train' on the Saturday, probably with more mail sacks than ever went in reality. As part of the celebrations a special set of railway letter stamps were issued and the first day covers were carried on this train. (Photo: Ian Drummond)

Below: The 'Mail Train' is seen leaving Dolgoch with *Talyllyn* in charge. (Photo: Darren Turner)

Above: There was an unexpected arrival at Tywyn Wharf on the Saturday afternoon, hiding away at the back of this photo is Talyllyn No.3 *Sir Haydn*, which, although out of service as its boiler certificate had expired, was brought down from Pendre works to join in the celebrations. (Photo: Ian Drummond)

Above: On the Saturday evening another cavalcade is being prepared at Tywyn Wharf, with all six of the Talyllyn's steam locomotives in view, including No.3 *Sir Haydn*. The six were to be at the head of a special evening train between Tywyn Wharf and Pendre where four of the locomotives were detached, leaving *Talyllyn* and *Dolgoch* to take the train up to Nant Gwernol and back to Wharf.   (Photo: Ian Drummond)

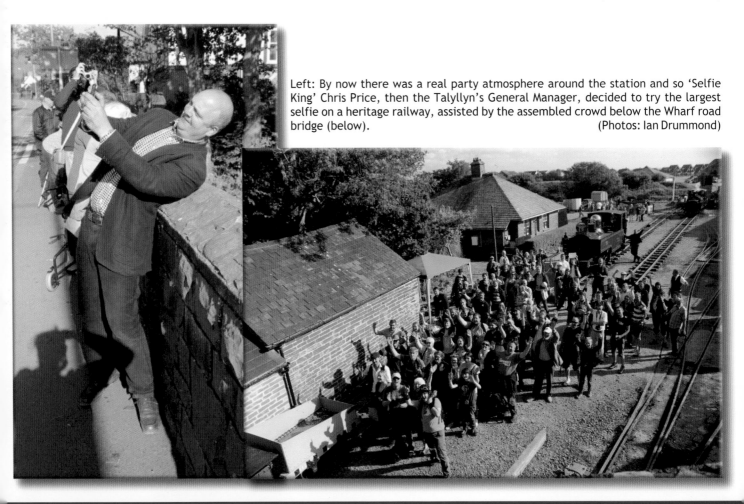

Left: By now there was a real party atmosphere around the station and so 'Selfie King' Chris Price, then the Talyllyn's General Manager, decided to try the largest selfie on a heritage railway, assisted by the assembled crowd below the Wharf road bridge (below).   (Photos: Ian Drummond)

Later on the Saturday evening *Talyllyn* and *Dolgoch* posed with *Russell* and *Prince* in the fading light at Tywyn Wharf. Here, with the aid of some floodlights, people were able to get a stunning set of photographs of these four iconic steam locomotives together for the first time.

(Photos:
Left: David J. Mitchell
Below and bottom: Ian Drummond)

Left: Early on the Sunday morning there was another photographic special this time involving No.2 *Dolgoch* and the vintage carriages, which is seen here on Brynglas bank. (Photo: David J. Mitchell)

Right: How many *Talyllyn's* can you see here? The annual Llechfan Garden Railway gala was also taking place during the weekend, and several people brought along models of Talyllyn Railway locomotives including this fine collection of *Talyllyns*. (Photo: Andrew Young)

Left: One of the re-enactments of the 150th Party was the last pre-preservation public passenger train, which originally ran on 6 October 1950, consisting of a single carriage and the brake van pulled by *Dolgoch*. Here the returning train can be seen at Tywyn Pendre on Sunday 5 July 2015. The fireman is Andrew Robinson and the guard Alex Hawesby. (Photo: Andrew Young)

Left: One of the joys of the Talyllyn 150 events was the little personal stories than came to light. The car in the photo had been driven to the Centenary celebrations in 1965, and both it and its owner made it to the 150th Party in July 2015.
(Photo: Andrew Young)

Right: Seen through the round window, or at least *Talyllyn's* spectacle plate, is *Dolgoch* entering Abergynolwyn on 3 July 2015.
(Photo: Andrew Young)

Below: Other talents were on display as well, Dolgoch station was 'yarn-bombed', with the nameboard well adorned as Marc Smith stands on the footplate of *Talyllyn*.
(Photo: Andrew Young)

The 1865 - 2015 Gala
7 - 9 August 2015

'The 1865 - 2015 Gala' took place at the height of the peak season, and so was designed with a family audience in mind with a series of 'themed days'. The first was a children's day based around 'Alice in Wonderland' which was originally published on 4 July 1865, the day before the Talyllyn Railway Act received its Royal Assent.

Left: No.6 masquerading as *Duncan* operating an Alice Shuttle train at Abergynolwyn.   (Photo: Darren Turner)

Right: Inevitably the Mad Hatter appeared, and worryingly he seemed intent on driving off with one of our locos.   (Photo: Darren Turner)

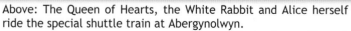

Above: The Queen of Hearts, the White Rabbit and Alice herself ride the special shuttle train at Abergynolwyn.
(Photo: Darren Turner)

Right: The White Rabbit also appeared to be at home on No.6's footplate.   (Photo: David J. Mitchell)

Left: The 'Breezy Special' proved to be an accidental renactment. It started with the idea of just running a fun train with all the open carriages together. However, there was then the chance discovery of a photo (below) in the archives of a train which ran on 22 August 1957, and so it became a re-creation. The train was assembled at Wharf in the early evening at Tywyn Wharf on 7 August 2015. It then set off with a full load of passengers to enjoy a beautiful evening ride up the valley headed by No.4 *Edward Thomas* with driver Bill Heynes in charge.
(Photo: Barbara Fuller)

Right: The original 'Breezy Special' on 22 August 1957. Note that then the opens did not have roofs.
(Photo: Keith Stretch)

Left: Saturday was 'Engineering Day' and down at Wharf station the gang was busy demonstrating what's involved in laying a section of track. At least one potential future volunteer seems to be taking a keen interest from their pushchair. (Photo: Darren Turner)

Right: Meanwhile tours were being offered of Pendre works, which could be reached by means of a special shuttle train from Tywyn Wharf with diesel No.9 *Alf* in charge. (Photo: Darren Turner)

Left: We also ran some special engineering trains reflecting different eras on the railway. Here No.2 *Dolgoch* departs from Tywyn Wharf with a train which could have been seen in the early 1950s when the preservation society first took over the railway.   (Photo: Ian Drummond)

Below: Later we ran a train which is typical of our present day operations, hauled by one of our two recently acquired Baguley diesels.   (Photo: David J. Mitchell)

Left: Not every special train we ran was for the galas. We also managed to fit in no fewer than three wedding trains during the course of the Talyllyn 150 galas. This is one of them about to depart from Tywyn Wharf on Saturday 8 August 2016.
                                                                (Photo: Ian Drummond)

Left: One of the aims of the galas was to have fun and that certainly happened on the Sunday, which was designated 1920s day, with many people entering into the spirit of the day. (Photo: Ian Drummond)

Right: However, perhaps some took things a little too far! (Photo: Ian Drummond)

Above: There was even jazz on the platform with a band who had given a concert at Neudd Pendre the evening before. This featured one of our drivers, John Scott, who can be seen busy blowing his own trombone. (Photo: Ian Drummond)

Right: Certainly some of our volunteers got in the mood as demonstrated by Emma Harrison and Becky Cottrell. (Photo: Ian Drummond)

Left: One of the special trains to run on the Sunday was the 'Farmers' Special', a mixed train with passenger coaches as well as wagons, which carried different types of goods to be delivered up and down the valley. The details of these deliveries had been discovered in the Talyllyn's archives. Sometimes livestock was transported along the line, however, in the intervening period since sheep were carried some of the staff's herding skills had been somewhat rusty, as John Smallwood demonstrates! Our 'sheep' made the return trip safely, although it was a bit stiff at the end, and was safely returned to its owners.   (Photo: Ian Drummond)

Below: The 'Farmers' Special' departs from Tywyn Wharf with *Talyllyn* in charge. Later it was to return with all the deliveries and collections made.   (Photo: Ian Drummond)

Left: In the afternoon a 1920s passenger train was run, which departed from one of the non-platform roads at Tywyn Wharf, a reminder that Wharf had no platforms before the 1950s when the preservation society took over. Instead passengers had to board the train making use of the footboards.
(Photo: Ian Drummond)

The Heart of Gold Weekend
29 - 31 August 2015

For the 'Heart of Gold Weekend', which was held over the August Bank Holiday, the emphasis shifted to the preservation era on the railway. However, first we looked ahead on the Saturday as it was the Young Members' Group day. This then led into an all-night steam event, before the Sunday and Monday had a 1950s feel.

Left: No.1 *Talyllyn* stands at Wharf Station with a Young Members' Special - Talyllyn 150 headboard. As many duties as possible were filled by those from the Young Members' Group during the Saturday and Sunday. This emphasised the vital role our young people play in the life of the railway, and indeed hopefully many of them will be around to celebrate Talyllyn 200!
(Photo: Darren Turner)

Right: As the sun set in the west *Dolgoch* stands at Wharf station ready for the 7.55 pm departure, as the all-night steam got under way. The train carried a special headboard to mark the 50th Anniversary of the Traffic and Operating Committee, which started in the Centenary year of 1965, and several past and present members of the group were on board.
(Photo: Barbara Fuller)

Left: Slightly earlier *Talyllyn* was seen approaching Brynglas with the Vintage Train, which ran throughout the night.
(Photo; Andrew Young)

Left: As day turns to night the railway takes on a new feel such as the interior of the shed at Pendre as engines were serviced throughout the hours of darkness. Here No.6 *Douglas* is being prepared for its next duty. (Photo: Andrew Young)

Right: Night running demands special measures. This neat idea gives a low level on light on the footplate sufficient to see gauges, without affecting the driver's night vision. (Photo: Andrew Young)

Left: Again night running gives a different atmosphere as seen here in Abergynolwyn blockpost where David Rowbotham is in charge.
(Photo: Andrew Young)

Left: Meanwhile down at Wharf station *Talyllyn* prepares to leave with the 9.55 pm departure. The trains were well patronised into the small hours, with many people taking advantage of the bar at Abergynolwyn en-route.
(Photo: David J. Mitchell)

Right: Later No.4 *Edward Thomas* is on shed being serviced with volunteers Chris Smith and Mike Brady; again the night gives a completely different feeling to the scene.
(Photo: Barbara Fuller)

Left: More atmosphere at Pendre station in the early hours where No.4 *Edward Thomas* now has the Young Members' Special headboard.   (Photo: Andrew Young)

Left: Up the line at Dolgoch station watering the locos in the dark presents new challenges.
(Photo: Darren Turner)

Right: Some disco lights at Dolgoch gave for some interesting lighting effects with passing trains during the night.
(Photo: Darren Turner)

Left: The night coincided with a 'Super Moon' when the full moon appears larger than normal, and the clear skies meant people were able to see it at its best. Here is the old water column at Dolgoch illuminated by moonlight.
(Photo: Darren Turner)

Above: The night atmosphere once again as No.2 *Dolgoch* stands at Abergynolwyn with a down train.   (Photo: Darren Turner)

Above: As dawn began to break on the Sunday there was a re-enactment of one of the early Monday morning Quarrymen's Specials which departed at 5.55 am from Tywyn Wharf. It is seen here at Dolgoch, the light from the oil headlight still clearly to be seen.
(Photo: Barbara Fuller)

Above: With the surrounding hills it takes a while for the sun to percolate through into the valley and reach places like Nant Gwernol station. This photograph was taken well after 9 am, and the sun is only now beginning to cast shadows across No.2 *Dolgoch* as it stands in the station. (Photo: Andrew Young)

Right: Running trains through the night is tremendous fun, but it is a lot of hard work and by the next morning it had all become too much for some. (Photo: Barbara Fuller)

Above: However, the Talyllyn doesn't rest and Sunday was 1950s day. At Tywyn Wharf there was the annual Series One Landrover display to add to the 1950s atmosphere. No.6 *Douglas* is admired by some young fans as it is prepared for the 12.15 pm departure. (Photo: Andrew Young)

Above: Again people entered into the spirit of the occasion and here Shop Supervisor, Kes Jones, adds to the atmosphere with her choice of costume. The Landrover also dates from the 1950s despite the 1963 numberplate. (Photo: Darren Turner)

Above: Again as part of the day there was a re-enactment of the railway's 'Coronation Train' originally run on 2 June 1953 to mark the Queen's Coronation that day. Once again we were able to run the original locomotive and rolling stock that were used on that occasion.   (Photo: David J. Mitchell)

Right: Here Morgan Price adds the original headboard to the decorated train at Tywyn Wharf before it departs.   (Photo: David J. Mitchell)

Above: The train departs to the delight of the assembled photographers.   (Photo: Barbara Fuller)

Above: Another special train that ran on the Sunday again reflecting the 1950s, was one of the 'express' services that operated in the late 1950s and into the 1960s. These only stopped at Dolgoch on their way to and from Abergynolwyn and carried a special headboard. Here No.4 *Edward Thomas* waits to depart from Tywyn Wharf with one of the original headboards.
(Photo: Ian Drummond)

Right: Also for a time in the 1950s it was the custom for guards to wear white coats. Here Holly Parrott is recreating the scene as she guards the 'Coronation Special'.
(Photo: Ian Drummond)

Left: One of the other attractions over the weekend was the presence of a London Routemaster bus. On the Saturday this had operated services between Abergynolwyn station and Talyllyn lake, then on the Sunday it had run between Tywyn and Fairbourne to allow passengers to ride on both the Talyllyn and Fairbourne Railways. On the Monday it ran along the valley road parallel to the railway so passengers could see the train from a new perspective. It is seen here on the Saturday making its way through Abergynolwyn village, probably to the great surprise of some of the locals!
(Photo: David J. Mitchell)

Left: One of the significant events in the life of the railway in the late 1950s was a major landslip near Dolgoch, which took many years to sort. During this time frequent trains of tipper wagons ran to the site taking spoil to be tipped into the void left by the slip. To commemorate the efforts of those involved a special train of tipper wagons hauled by diesel No.5 *Midlander* was run between Tywyn and Quarry Siding on the Monday. It is seen here being shunted at Tywyn Wharf with Chris Johnson in charge.
(Photo: Ian Drummond)

Right: One of the last trains of the gala was another 'fun' train. The 'No.7 Special' consisted of locomotive No.7 *Tom Rolt* and every item of rolling stock with a seven in its number. Hence the train consisted of carriages Nos. 7 and 17 with engineering van No.70. It is seen here at Pendre with driver Bill Tyndall at the regulator.
(Photo: Barbara Fuller)

Left: A poignant moment. Chris Price was about to enter his last month as General Manager of the Talyllyn Railway. At the end of the Monday he realised that one thing he had never done on the railway was to accept a token at Wharf station, so here he is accepting the token from Andrew Vick as No.4 *Edward Thomas* enters the station.
(Photo: Ian Drummond)

The Heritage Weekend
25 - 27 September 2015

Left: 'The Heritage Weekend' gala was combined with the TRPS Annual General Meeting and was very much focused on a celebration for members and enthusiasts. It started on the Friday with the departure of the 'Day Rover'. Up until 1995 a return ticket simply entitled a passenger to a single journey up and down the line. However, in 1995 for an extra £1 you could upgrade your return ticket to a day rover to allow you to spend the day on the railway. Later this was extended to all full return tickets. This train was designed to give a full value day out on the railway with a six hour excursion running round at all the passing loops on the line in both directions before arriving back at Tywyn. So at 9.30 am some keen passengers embarked on their day trip.   (Photo: Ian Drummond)

Right: At various times since the preservation society took over the Talyllyn has run Fridays only winter shoppers' specials between Rhydyronen or Brynglas and Tywyn to serve the local community. These finally ended in the 1970s. However for this gala it was decided to re-create the 1960s incarnation of the shoppers' special which often consisted of diesel loco No.5 *Midlander* with Corris carriage No.17 and Corris van No.6. It is seen here at Pendre station ready to depart with David Martin at the controls of No.5 on Friday 25 September 2015. There is even a genuine shopper boarding the train!
                (Photo: Ian Drummond)

Left: The weather was glorious throughout the weekend and here the shoppers' special has run round at Brynglas ready for its return trip back to Tywyn.
                (Photo: Ian Drummond)

Left: Later on the Friday No.2 *Dolgoch* was in charge of the vintage set for 'The Last, Last Pre-preservation Train'. The last timetabled public train before preservation ran in October 1950. However, a little known fact is that at least one more passenger train was run before the preservation society took over. This was in late 1950 for the benefit of the members of the first committee of the TRPS to view the line, as some of the group had not visited the railway up until this point. The train is seen here taking water at Dolgoch. (Photo: Darren Turner)

Right: The train departs from Dolgoch and heads towards Quarry Siding. (Photo: Darren Turner)

Left: Meanwhile No.1 *Talyllyn* was heading one of the service trains and is seen here heading back down to Tywyn across the viaduct at Dolgoch. (Photo: Darren Turner)

Left: While all this was going on 'The Day Rover' continued its journey up and down the line running round at various locations, such as here at Brynglas with blockman Gethin Taylor looking on. It finally returned to Tywyn Wharf just after 4 pm.

(Photo: Ian Drummond)

Right and Below: Later on the Friday evening there was another evening photoshoot involving Nos. 1 and 2 at Tywyn Wharf. (Photos: David J. Mitchell)

Left: The Saturday morning dawned bright for the 'Sunrise Saloon Special', which consisted of all the railways saloon carriages running as one train set. As the train ran up the valley the sun gradually began to light up the hills.   (Photo: Ian Drummond)

Right: The idea was that the train should get to Nant Gwernol at 7.55 am just as the sun lit up the station. Unfortunately our timing was a bit out and although many of the surrounding hills were bathed in sunlight, the station remained in shadow while the train crew ran No.1 *Talyllyn* round the train.
(Photo: Ian Drummond)

Left: At Dolgoch on the down trip the train paused for the loco to take on more water. It was still in the shade at this time.   (Photo: Ian Drummond)

Right: However, at Brynglas the sun finally illuminated the train bringing a smile to everyone's face including driver Viv Thorpe. Note that former Corris carriage No.17 is unusually marshalled at the west end of the train.   (Photo: Ian Drummond)

Above: Later on the Saturday there was a re-run of 'The Sesquicentenarian' for those members who had missed the original running in July. It is seen here at Tywyn Wharf getting ready to depart. (Photo: David J. Mitchell)

Above: The train is now seen departing from Dolgoch with the dappled sunlight streaming through the trees.
(Photo: Darren Turner)

Above: Another special train that was run on the Saturday was the 'Royal Train'. This consisted of all the locos and rolling stock which had featured in our two royal visits by the Prince of Wales, first with Princess Diana in 1982 and then with the Duchess of Cornwall in 2005. It consisted of locos No.2 *Dolgoch* and No.7 *Tom Rolt* along with ex-Corris carriage No. 17; saloon coach No.20 and brake van No.16. It ran from Tywyn Wharf to Brynglas where it ran round, as seen here from the sky, giving a new perspective on the railway.

(Photo: Darren Turner)

Right: Then it was a case of the train crew having to wait for appropriate departure time in Brynglas station.

(Photo: Darren Turner)

Left: Finally blockman Andrew Young allows them to depart for Tywyn.
(Photo: Darren Turner)

The Saturday evening was taken up with the Society AGM at the cinema in Tywyn. This was followed by the showing of some vintage Talyllyn films, concluding with a screening of *The Titfield Thunderbolt*. The Ealing Comedy inspired by the story of the Talyllyn and drawing on many aspects and stories from the early days of the preserved railway.

Right: Then on the Sunday morning a special ceremony took place at the Brynglas Memorial Garden to commemorate all those who had worked on the railway during its 150 years. This included a minute's silence, the conclusion of which was marked by the sounding of *Talyllyn's* whistle, a sound which had echoed across the valley for all those years.

(Photo: David J. Mitchell)

Left: Later both No.1 and No.2 were back out on the line, running separate trains; one with the vintage carriage set and the other with the vintage wagons up the line. These were then combined into a long mixed train for the down journey. They are seen here on the down train between Abergynolwyn and Quarry Siding.

(Photo: David J. Mitchell)

Right: Then the train is seen passing Rhydyronen, with the LV (Last Vehicle) board appropriately marking the conclusion of the 2015 galas.

(Photo: David J. Mitchell)

The Road to Adventure Gala
30 April - 2 May 2016

Above: The day before the start of 'The Road to Adventure' gala there was the opportunity to take photographs of some special visitors. Tim and Richard Rolt, Tom Rolt's two sons, came down for the gala and brought one of their father's Alvis cars with them. Tim is seen at Tywyn Wharf on the footplate of No.2 *Dolgoch*, the Old Lady, as Tom Rolt called it in his book *Railway Adventure*, while Richard Rolt is seen at the wheel of his father's Alvis. (Photo: Ian Drummond)

Above: Then there was the chance to photograph No.7 *Tom Rolt* next to Tom's Alvis. (Photo: Ian Drummond)

Above: The weekend was a back to the 1970s event, and on the Saturday we ran a modified version of the peak 1975 timetable. Here at Tywyn Wharf the first train of the day gets under way, with Mike Davies at the regulator of No.4 *Edward Thomas*.   (Photo: Ian Drummond)

Right: Of course in 1975 passenger trains only ran as far as Abergynolwyn as the extension to Nant Gwernol wasn't opened until the following year. This meant that at Abergynolwyn gala passengers had to change trains to a special shuttle train which ran to Nant Gwernol topped and tailed by No.7 *Tom Rolt* and diesel No.9 *Alf*. By this time though the weather was beginning to deteriorate, but it doesn't seem to bother Chris Palmer on *Alf*, while Andy Vick is at the controls.
(Photo: Ian Drummond)

The Road to Adventure Gala was centred around the opening of the extension between Abergynolwyn and Nant Gwernol on 22 May 1976. Originally this had just been used for mineral trains, and had been out of regular use for some time when the preservation society took over in 1951. However, it was always Tom Rolt's dream to open the line to passenger trains along what he dubbed 'The Road to Adventure'.

Above: Finally on 3 October 1970 Tom Rolt detonated the first blast to start widening the trackbed from Abergynolwyn ready for passenger trains. On Saturday 30 April 2016 Tim and Richard Rolt were present to re-create this event with the aid of some large fireworks to simulate the blast. (Photo: Barbara Fuller)

Above: At Abergynolwyn the 1970s theme was 'Abba at Aber' with a range of Abba railway themed items around the station. (Photo: Diane Drummond)

Left: The 1970s mood continued with an evening disco at Tywyn Wharf. Some members are seen here getting well into the 1970s groove (left to right) Kes Jones, Shirley Washbrook and Lorraine Simkiss. (Photo: Ian Drummond)

Right: If we thought the rain for 'The Quarryman Experience' gala the previous year was bad, we had yet to experience that which arrived for Sunday 1 May 2016 when we celebrated the opening to Nant Gwernol, with a re-enactment of the opening train. Here No.2 *Dolgoch* stands at Tywyn Wharf station complete with the original opening headboard ready for the trip to Nant Gwernol.

(Photo: Ian Drummond)

Left: At Abergynolwyn there was a photo opportunity which featured some of those who had been active on the railway in the 1970s. This included some of the original 'Gwerns' who had been responsible for building the extension. The ribbon shown in the photo is also the original one from the opening in 1976. By now the weather was distinctly inclement.

(Photo: Ian Drummond)

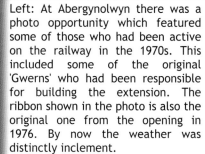

Right: By the time the train got to Nant Gwernol the weather was even worse, and the headboard had to be rescued before it got waterlogged.
(Photo: Ian Drummond)

Above: As stated previously some of those originally involved on the railway in the 1970s were around for the weekend. This included Michael Howard, who was the guard on the original opening train and is giving the right of way at Abergynolwyn 40 years later. (Photo: Ian Drummond)

Above: Driving the original opening train was Dai Jones with Phil Guest as the fireman. In 2016 it was Dai's son David at the regulator of No.2 seen here on the left with fireman Nick Fieldhouse on the right. (Photo: Keith Theobald)

Above Left: Back at Abergynolwyn there was a short ceremony to mark the 40th Anniversary of the opening including three of the stalwarts of the railway in the 1970s with Jane Garvey Chairman of the TRPS on the left, then there is Bob Gunn who was in charge of much of the construction work on the extension, then David Woodhouse, Traffic and later General Manager of the railway, and finally Richard Hope for many years Secretary of the Society. (Photo: Ian Drummond)

Right: Then Bob Gunn cuts a celebration cake aided by Jane Garvey, with the original golden spike also on display. (Photo: David J. Mitchell)

Left: On the Bank Holiday Monday there were two other celebrations. The first was to mark the 25th Anniversary of the railway's newest steam locomotive No.7 *Tom Rolt*. As part of the celebrations it was out early on the Monday morning with a photographic train seen here at Rhydyronen, with its special headboard.
(Photo: David J. Mitchell)

Right: The opportunity was taken for some special shots including this one of No.7 bursting through arch of the bridge at Brynglas with driver Bill Tyndall at the regulator.   (Photo: David J. Mitchell)

Left: Later No.7 was in charge of a special train, which is seen here on arrival at Abergynolwyn, the scene of its original commissioning 25 years before. David Jones is on the footplate with Mike Green, who had been involved in the construction of No.7, beside it on the platform.
(Photo: David J. Mitchell)

Left: The other celebration was to mark the 75th Anniversary of diesel No.5 *Midlander* seen here at Tywyn Wharf with driver Rob Frost (left), who was responsible for much of its rebuild, and Interim Managing Director David Ventry (right). It had been given charge of the vintage set for the day. (Photo: Ian Drummond)

Right: At Abergynolwyn the two locomotives with a combined age of 100 were brought six feet apart ready to mark their anniversaries. Tim (left) and Richard (right) Rolt then performed a short ceremony to mark the occasion. (Photo: David Churchill)

Below: After this John Bate, the designer of *Tom Rolt* and the railway's former chief engineer, cut a special celebration cake in front of the assembled photographers. (Photo: David Churchill)

Above: Another special moment as Rob Frost poses at Tywyn Wharf with Lawrie Ellis who was the first person to drive *Midlander* on Talyllyn rails.
(Photo: Ian Drummond)

Left: No.5 and its train then headed back towards Tywyn and is seen here approaching Brynglas.
(Photo: Barbara Fuller)

Right: At Brynglas No.5 and its train took part in a rare three way crossing with *Midlander* and carriages sitting in the siding while the service trains passed each other. (Photo: David Churchill)

Left: Then *Midlander* had to wait for the down train to clear the section. Note the starting handle ready to bring the locomotive back to life. (Photo: Ian Drummond)

The Grand Finale
1 - 3 July 2016

The success of the early galas in 2015 initiated thoughts as to how the 150th Anniversary events could be finished in style. A celebration of the 40th Anniversary of the opening to Nant Gwernol had already been mooted, which became 'The Road To Adventure' gala. However, what could we do to match the 150th Party? At this point in June 2015 the opportunity arose for the Narrow Gauge Railway Museum to acquire the Fletcher Jennings locomotive *William Finlay*. This led to the revival of an earlier idea of bringing together all of the five surviving UK-based Fletcher Jennings locomotives for the first time ever, and with that 'The Grand Finale' event was born.

Left: Aside from the Talyllyn's own *Talyllyn* and *Dolgoch* the other three surviving Fletcher Jennings locomotives had been built for the Dorking Greystone Company for its quarry at Betchworth. These included two locomotives constructed to the unusual gauge of 3 ft 2¼ in. As noted above *William Finlay* has been acquired by the Narrow Gauge Railway Museum, while its twin *Townsend Hook* was undergoing cosmetic restoration at Amberley Museum and Heritage Centre in West Sussex. Some very hard work by the volunteers there however, got *Townsend Hook* ready to be brought to the gala, and the two locomotives arrived together on one low-loader, to provide another 'Once In A Lifetime' sight at Tywyn Wharf.
(Photo: Keith Theobald)

Right: The third Betchworth locomotive was the standard gauge *Captain Baxter*, now based at the Bluebell Railway in East Sussex. Unlike *Townsend Hook* and *William Finlay* it is in working order and so could be steamed on a specially laid section of standard gauge track. Thus on Thursday 30 June there was a never before seen sight from the Neptune Road bridge at Tywyn Wharf of a standard gauge locomotive on Talyllyn property.
(Photo: Ian Drummond)

Left: By mid-afternoon on the Thursday the final preparations were well in hand for the gala. Even the beer tent had been erected! *Townsend Hook* stood on a short section of track in the distance, with the standard gauge track on which *Captain Baxter* would steam next to it. Then receiving final attention was *William Finlay*. Meanwhile a fourth Fletcher Jennings locomotive *Dolgoch* was running round its train.
(Photo: Ian Drummond)

Left: The celebratory focus of the weekend was *Dolgoch's* 150th Anniversary, and on the Friday of the gala a special headboard was revealed by Tim Dunn, one of the presenters on the BBC's *Trainspotting Live* and David Mitchell, President of the TRPS, at Wharf station. (Photo: Darren Turner)

Right: Three hundred years between the three of them, as posing in front of *Dolgoch* are Nigel Adams and John Smallwood. (Photo: David J. Mitchell)

Above: Then *Dolgoch* took a special train, with some of those who had donated to an appeal for a new boiler in 2010 run under the auspices of *Steam Railway* magazine, up the line. It is seen here passing Cynfal Halt. (Photo: Andrew Young)

Left: On the Friday evening *Dolgoch* was in charge of a special heritage train which stopped at various points along the line, such as here at Tŷ Mawr. This was to enable some of the railway's history to be explained to those on board.
(Photo: Andrew Young)

Right: National Railway Museum Senior Curator, Anthony Coulls, who was the fireman on the trip, takes a cold shower at Dolgoch as the loco takes water.
(Photo: Andrew Young)

Left: The train also paused at the site of the old winding house. (Photo: Andrew Young)

Above: Saturday very much echoed the previous year's 150th Party. It started with a line up of all the steamable locomotives at Wharf, which brought together the five Fletcher Jennings survivors for the first time. Left to right we have *Townsend Hook*, *Captain Baxter*, *Dolgoch*, *William Finlay* and *Talyllyn*. (Photo: Barbara Fuller)

Above: The view from Wharf bridge which also included No.4 *Edward Thomas*, No.6 *Douglas* and No.7 *Tom Rolt*.
(Photo: Ian Drummond)

Left: A unique Fletcher Jennings line up.
(Photo: Barbara Fuller)

Right: On the Saturday *Dolgoch's* 150th Anniversary was marked once more, with the cutting of another celebration cake. This time performed by new General Manager Tracey Parkinson, with TRPS Chairman Jane Garvey.   (Photo: Darren Turner)

Left: *Dolgoch* then took a special train up the valley, which included the usual stop at Dolgoch for water. However, the fireman on this trip has a trick to avoid getting wet, hanging a shovel on the operating handle of the water tower.

(Photo: Ian Drummond)

Right: Down at Wharf shunting is taking place to get a mixed train ready to go out, with *William Finlay* and *Captain Baxter* behind.
(Photo: David J. Mitchell)

Left: Saturday saw another evening train hauled by all the TR's steamable locos depart from Tywyn Wharf.
(Photo: David J. Mitchell)

Right: The train arrives at Pendre where the three leading locos were detached leaving *Talyllyn* and *Dolgoch* to take the train to Nant Gwernol.
(Photo: Barbara Fuller)

Left: After the locos had been detached trainee blockman Josh Green waits to give the green flag to the remaining section of the train to depart under the watchful gaze of blockman Barney Bell, while Liz Garvey looks on.
(Photo: Barbara Fuller)

Above: Later on Saturday evening the Fletcher Jennings locos were lined up again under the floodlights.

(Photo: Ian Drummond)

Left: The family similarity between (left to right) *Dolgoch, William Finlay* and *Talyllyn* is obvious from this photo.

(Photo: Barbara Fuller)

Below: The UK-based Lowca Legacy of locos produced at Lowca works can be seen again here.   (Photo: Ian Drummond)

Left: During the weekend *Captain Baxter* had been trundling up and down its length of track.
(Photo: Andrew Young)

Right: *Captain Baxter* also provided the opportunity for footplate rides which clearly delighted General Manager Tracey Parkinson who is on the footplate with Will Smith (left) and Andrew Bailey (right).
(Photo: Darren Turner)

Left: Sunday morning saw another photographic special this time involving *Dolgoch* with a mixed train, which is seen here departing from Dolgoch.
(Photo: David J. Mitchell)

Left: At Nant Gwernol *Dolgoch* shunts the train ready for its return journey under the watchful gaze of driver Bob Morland.
(Photo: David J. Mitchell)

Right: One of the important tasks with the vintage wagons is to keep the axleboxes well lubricated as Bob Morland is doing here.
(Photo: David J. Mitchell)

Left: Later the same morning *Dolgoch* linked up with *Talyllyn* to head the 'Fletcher Jennings Special', seen here passing Brynglas.
(Photo: Andrew Young)

Left: Over the weekend the Garden Railway was also having its annual gala again and here Kes Jones is seen with her latest pride and joy on the temporary 5 inch track. The loco is a model of a full size replica loco her father had once built in their back garden.   (Photo: David J. Mitchell)

Right: On the garden railway itself a model of a model village was opened by Tim Dunn, who has close links with the Beckonscot Model Village at Beaconsfield. Can you spot the model village within the model village?

(Photo: Ian Drummond)

Left: The last special train of the gala was a recreation of what the very first public passenger train might have looked like. This ran in December 1866 and probably consisted of locomotive *Dolgoch* with what are now carriages Nos. 3 and 4 and brake van No.5. How many railways could recreate their first train 150 years later? It is seen here at Rhydyronen. A full re-enactment of this train is due to take place on 16 December 2016.

(Photo: David J. Mitchell)

Left: All too soon it was time for the final train of the last gala in the Talyllyn 150th celebrations. At 3.45 pm on Sunday 3 July 2016 No.6 *Douglas* and No.1 *Talyllyn* depart from Tywyn Wharf for Nant Gwernol.

(Photo: Ian Drummond)

Below: Time to pack everything away, as the outdoor gang move in to take up the temporary track.

(Photo: Ian Drummond)